NEW ZEALAND
WEATHER

Written and Illustrated by
Alistair Hughes

WHITE CLOUD BOOKS

“I’ve always wanted to know what makes our weather tick, because when it’s good it’s great, but when it turns it can be pretty wicked.”

Gus Roxburgh,
NZ film director

In Aotearoa New Zealand, we usually tell visitors that we have 'good' weather. But what does that mean, and what causes 'bad' weather: clouds to form, rain to fall or even lightning to strike?

Our island nation lies almost midway between the tropics and the Antarctic. Sometimes, we are warmed by hot air from the tropics and at other times chilled by cold polar air from the south. Most of the time, New Zealand experiences prevailing westerly wind, which can cause our changeable weather.

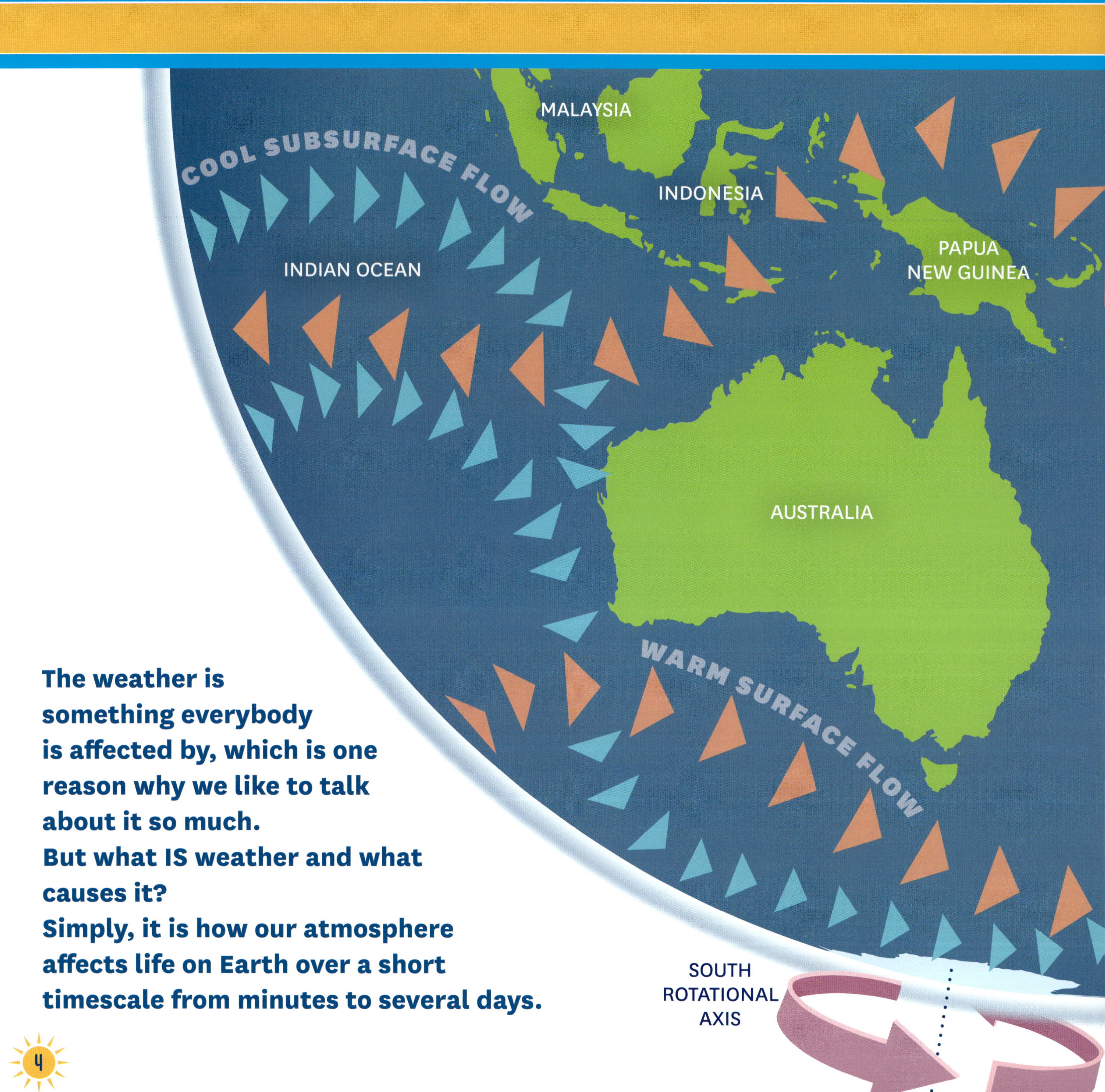

The weather is something everybody is affected by, which is one reason why we like to talk about it so much.

But what IS weather and what causes it?

Simply, it is how our atmosphere affects life on Earth over a short timescale from minutes to several days.

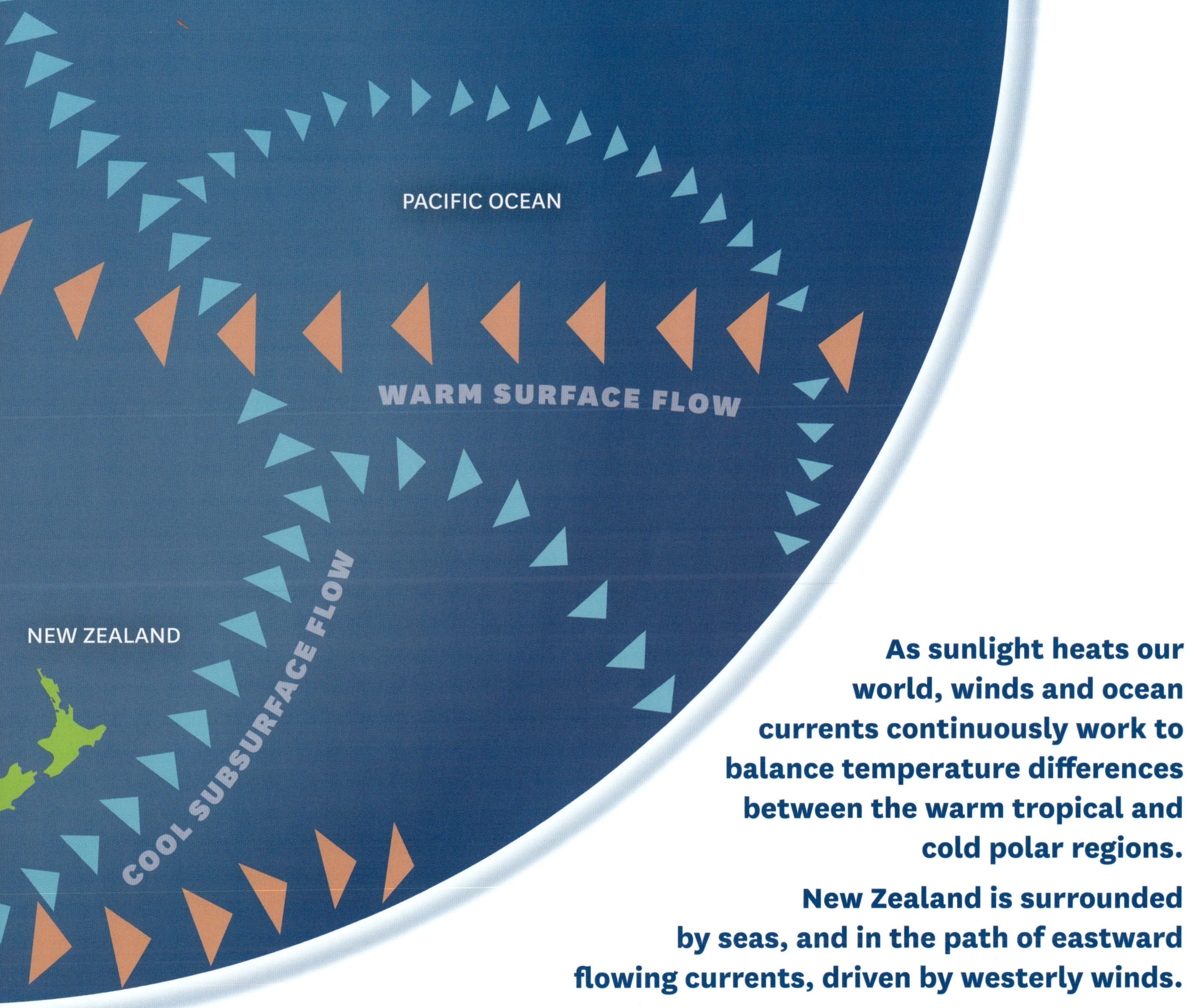

As sunlight heats our world, winds and ocean currents continuously work to balance temperature differences between the warm tropical and cold polar regions.

New Zealand is surrounded by seas, and in the path of eastward flowing currents, driven by westerly winds.

LAND OF THE LONG WET COLD?

When the East Polynesian ancestors of Māori first arrived in New Zealand, they found a colder climate (long-term pattern of weather), than the tropical one they had left behind.

Some plants they had brought for weaving of bark cloth garments did not grow well, so they adapted their skills to what was available.

Aotearoa's cooler, wetter conditions required changes to traditional methods of fishing, hunting and growing crops. The kūmara they brought with them now needed raised garden beds and drainage because of rain.

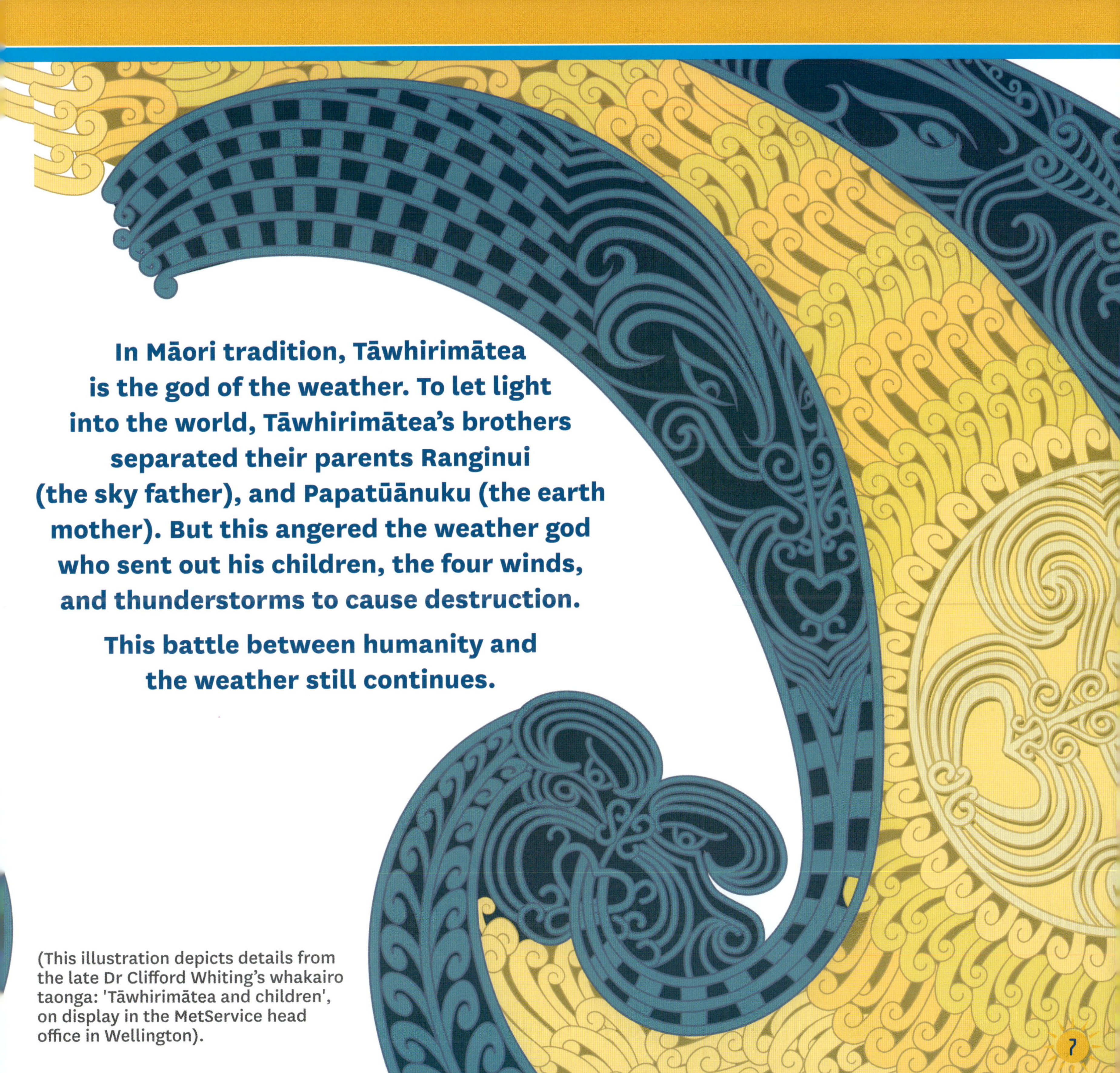

In Māori tradition, Tāwhirimātea is the god of the weather. To let light into the world, Tāwhirimātea's brothers separated their parents Ranginui (the sky father), and Papatūānuku (the earth mother). But this angered the weather god who sent out his children, the four winds, and thunderstorms to cause destruction.

This battle between humanity and the weather still continues.

(This illustration depicts details from the late Dr Clifford Whiting's whakairo taonga: 'Tāwhirimātea and children', on display in the MetService head office in Wellington).

In New Zealand, winds most commonly blow from a westerly direction. This means that our weather tends to pass from west to east across the country.

Gusts over 120 km per hour can blow trees over and vehicles off the road.

Northerlies and northwesterlies bring warm moist air which has moved across tropical or subtropical oceans, and often Australia's heated land mass. Some of New Zealand's highest rainfalls, and highest temperatures recorded, occurred during northerly or northwest conditions.

The west coasts of the North and South Islands face into the westerly flow, while the east coasts are protected from it by mountain ranges. This is why the climate is generally cooler and wetter in western parts of New Zealand, and warmer and drier in the east.

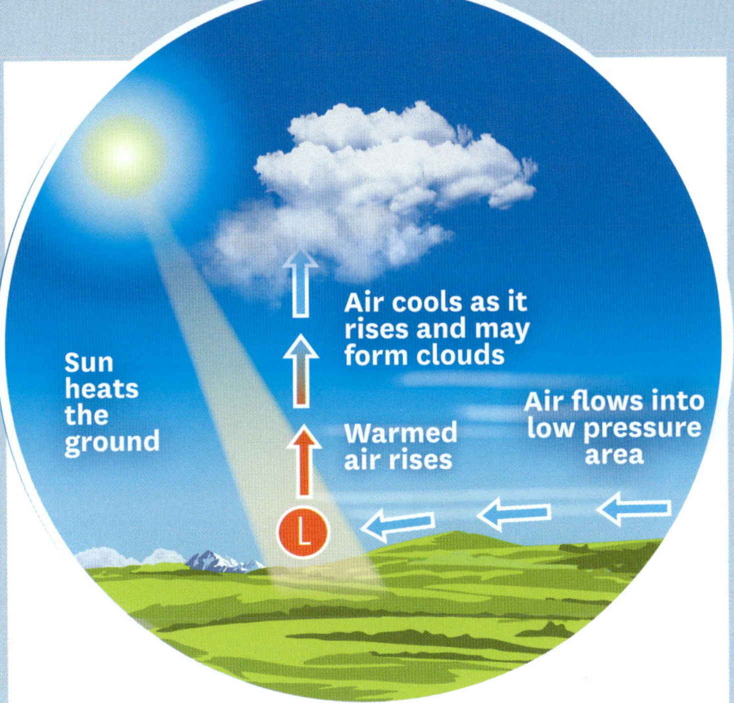

Wind is the movement of air from one place to another. The sun's uneven heating of the Earth's surface raises a particular area's temperature, causing air to rise and leave behind a pocket of low atmospheric pressure, which is rapidly filled by surrounding higher pressure air.

This air movement is further influenced by friction between air and land, and the force of the Earth's rotation.

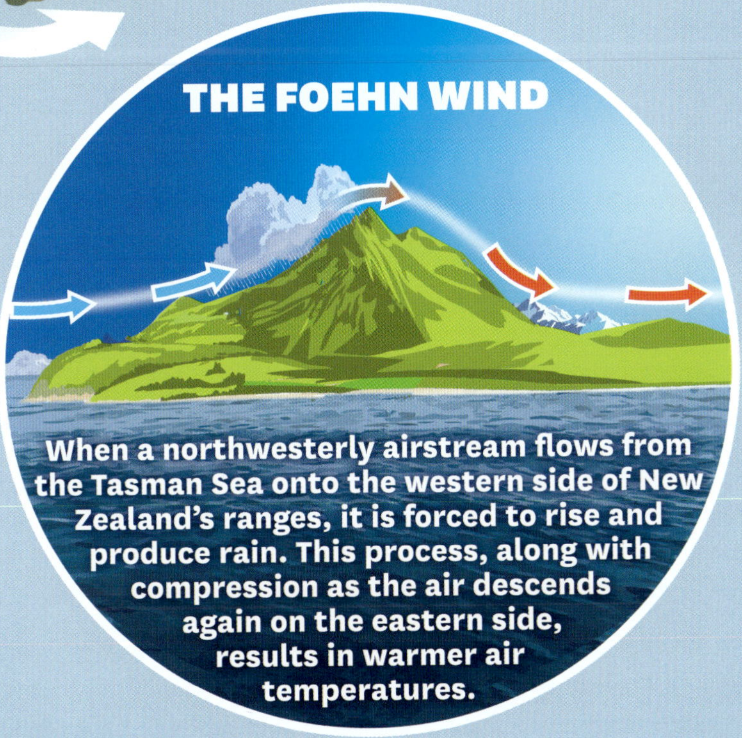

THE FOEHN WIND

When a northwesterly airstream flows from the Tasman Sea onto the western side of New Zealand's ranges, it is forced to rise and produce rain. This process, along with compression as the air descends again on the eastern side, results in warmer air temperatures.

In the tropical South Pacific, easterly winds (called the 'trade winds'), push sea water west, heated by sunlight and resulting in a region of warmer ocean. Meanwhile, off the west coast of South America, colder currents replace the warm water that has been moved away.

This interaction between the atmosphere and ocean in the tropical Pacific is known as the *Southern Oscillation*. *El Niño* and *La Niña* are opposing phases of this climate cycle and affect the seasonal weather patterns of several countries, including our own.

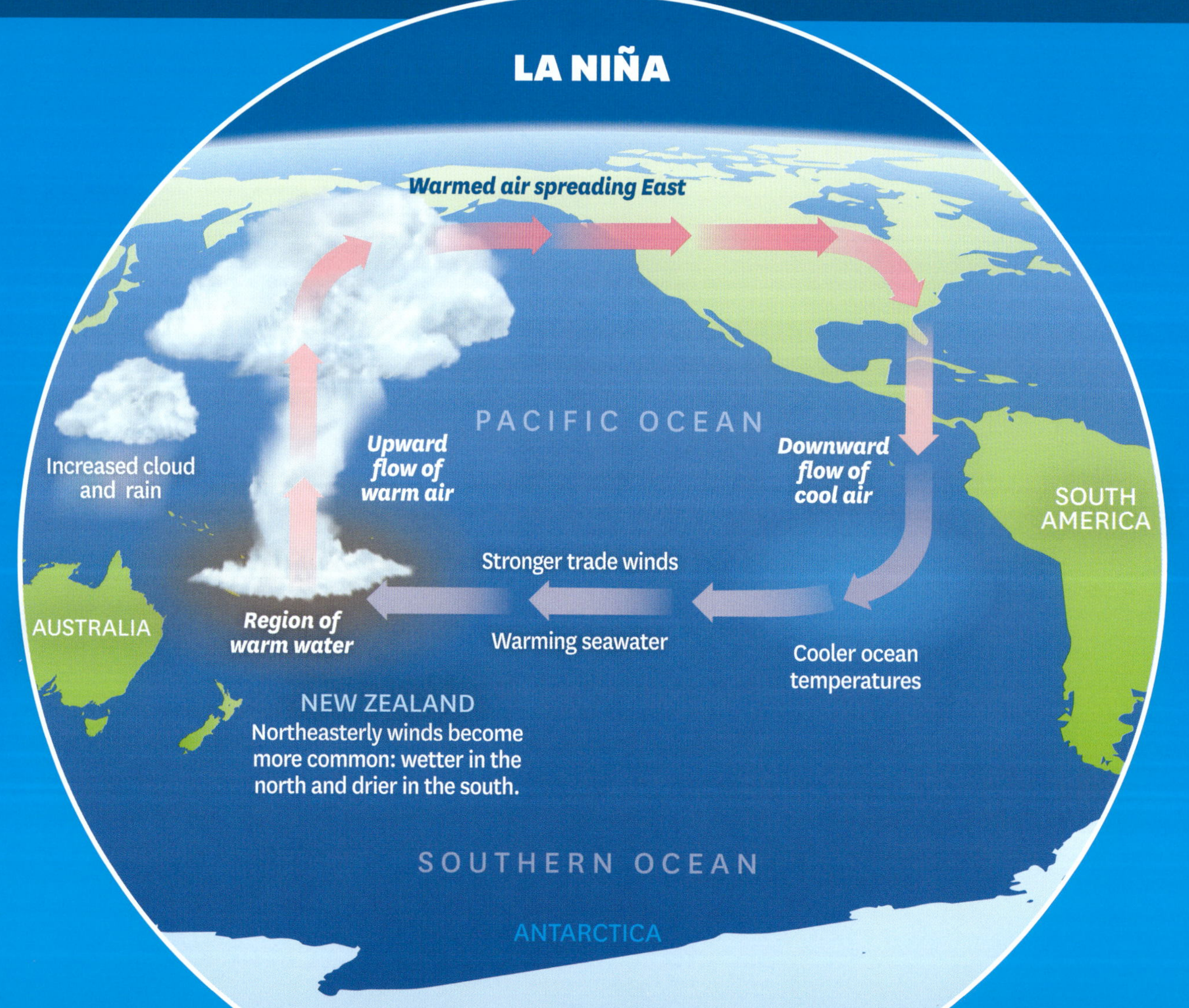

During *La Niña*, the easterly trade winds strengthen, causing a greater build-up of warm sea water in the western Pacific. This brings more tropical clouds and rain. Meanwhile, cooler, deep seawater rises as the trade winds churn the ocean surface off the South American coast.

When *El Niño takes place*, the easterly trade winds weaken or reverse, and warmer regions of sea water build up on the opposite side of the ocean, near South America. This shifts tropical cloud and rain westward into the Pacific and results in cooler western ocean temperatures.

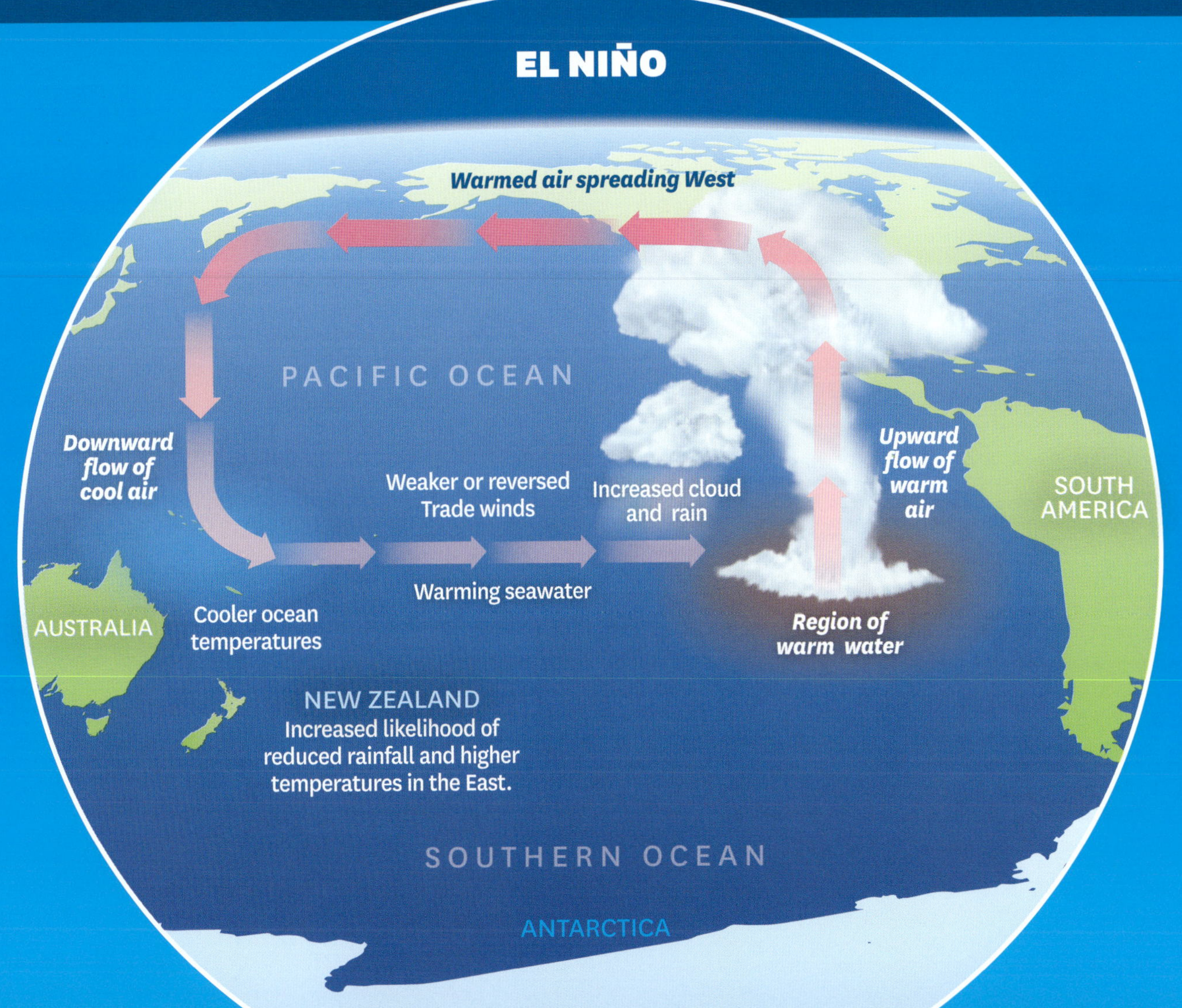

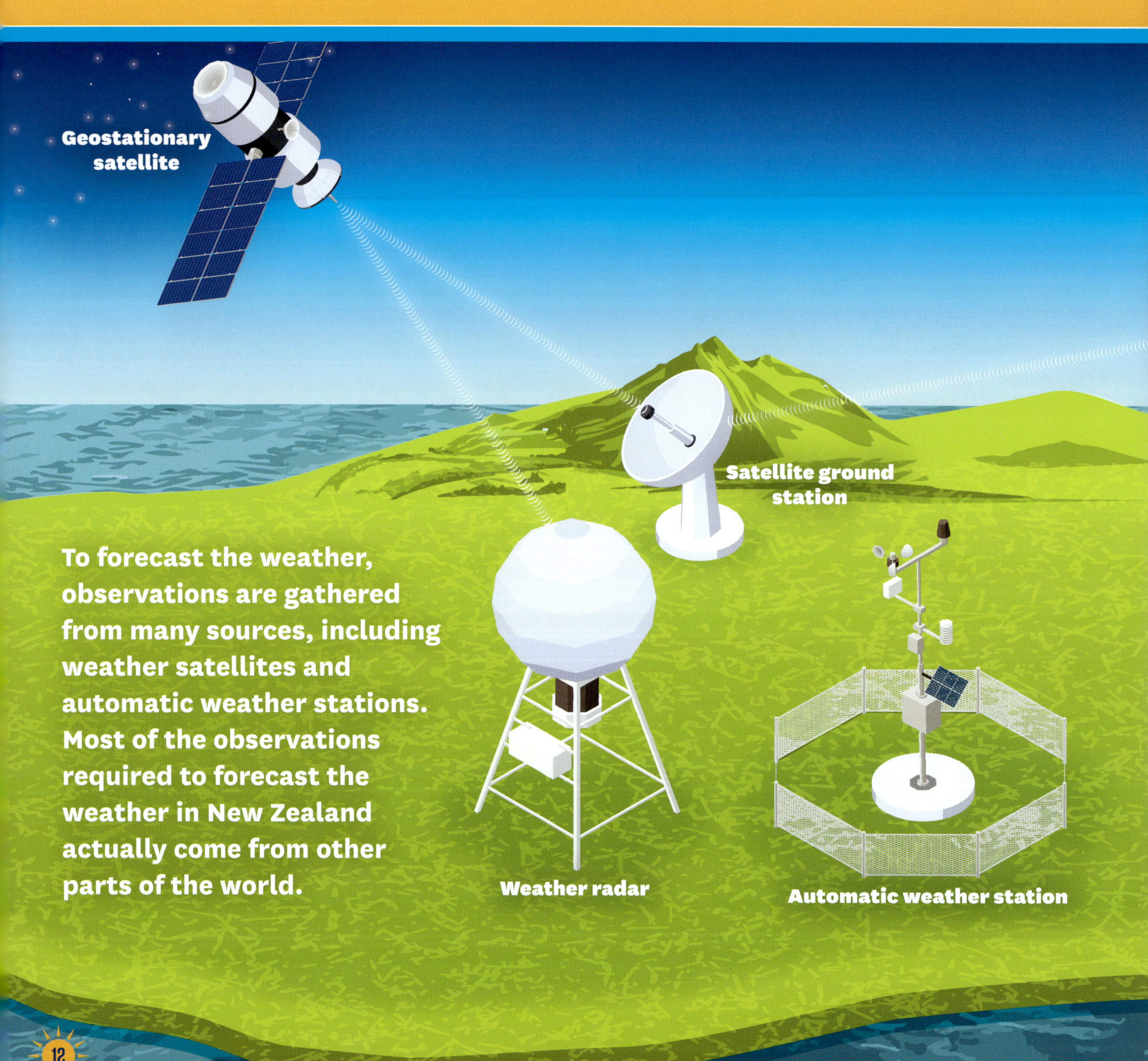

To forecast the weather, observations are gathered from many sources, including weather satellites and automatic weather stations. Most of the observations required to forecast the weather in New Zealand actually come from other parts of the world.

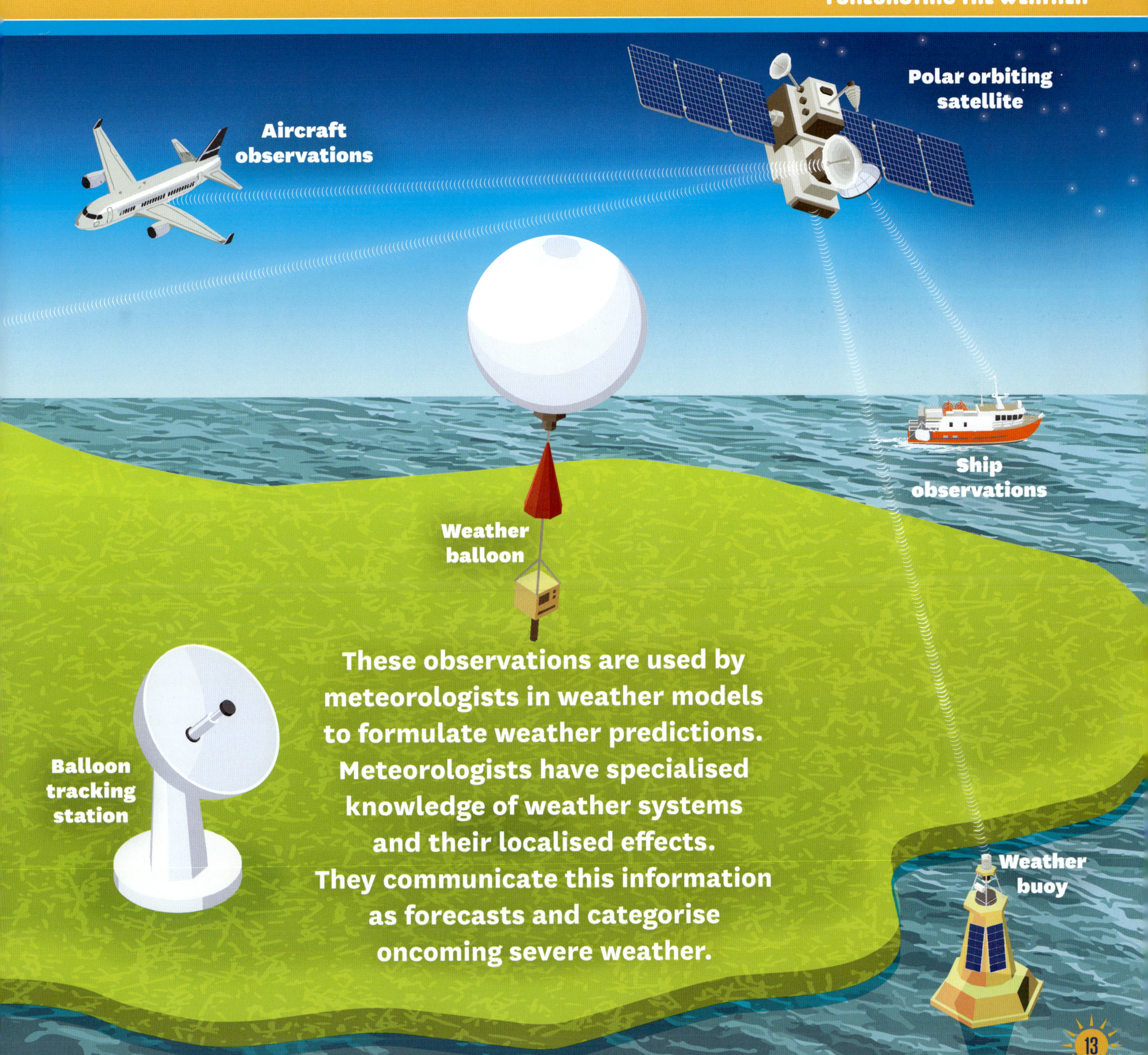

These observations are used by meteorologists in weather models to formulate weather predictions. Meteorologists have specialised knowledge of weather systems and their localised effects. They communicate this information as forecasts and categorise oncoming severe weather.

H
HIGH
Highs are regions of air spiralling outwards in an anti clockwise direction, with light winds near their centres and typically bring clear skies or some low cloud.

L
LOW
Lows are regions of air spiralling outwards in a clockwise direction, bringing changeable, (but generally wet and windy), weather.

WARM FRONT
A warm front is the edge of a moving mass of warm air. It is usually accompanied by a band of rain.

COLD FRONT
A cold front is the edge of a moving mass of cold air, often accompanied by a band of heavy showers.

STATIONARY FRONT
A very slow moving warm or cold front.

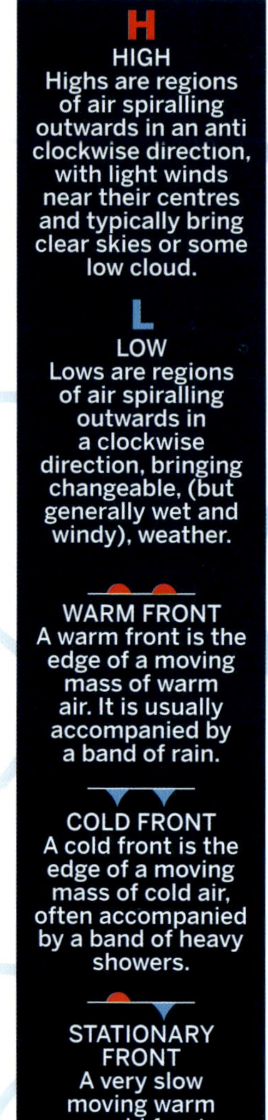

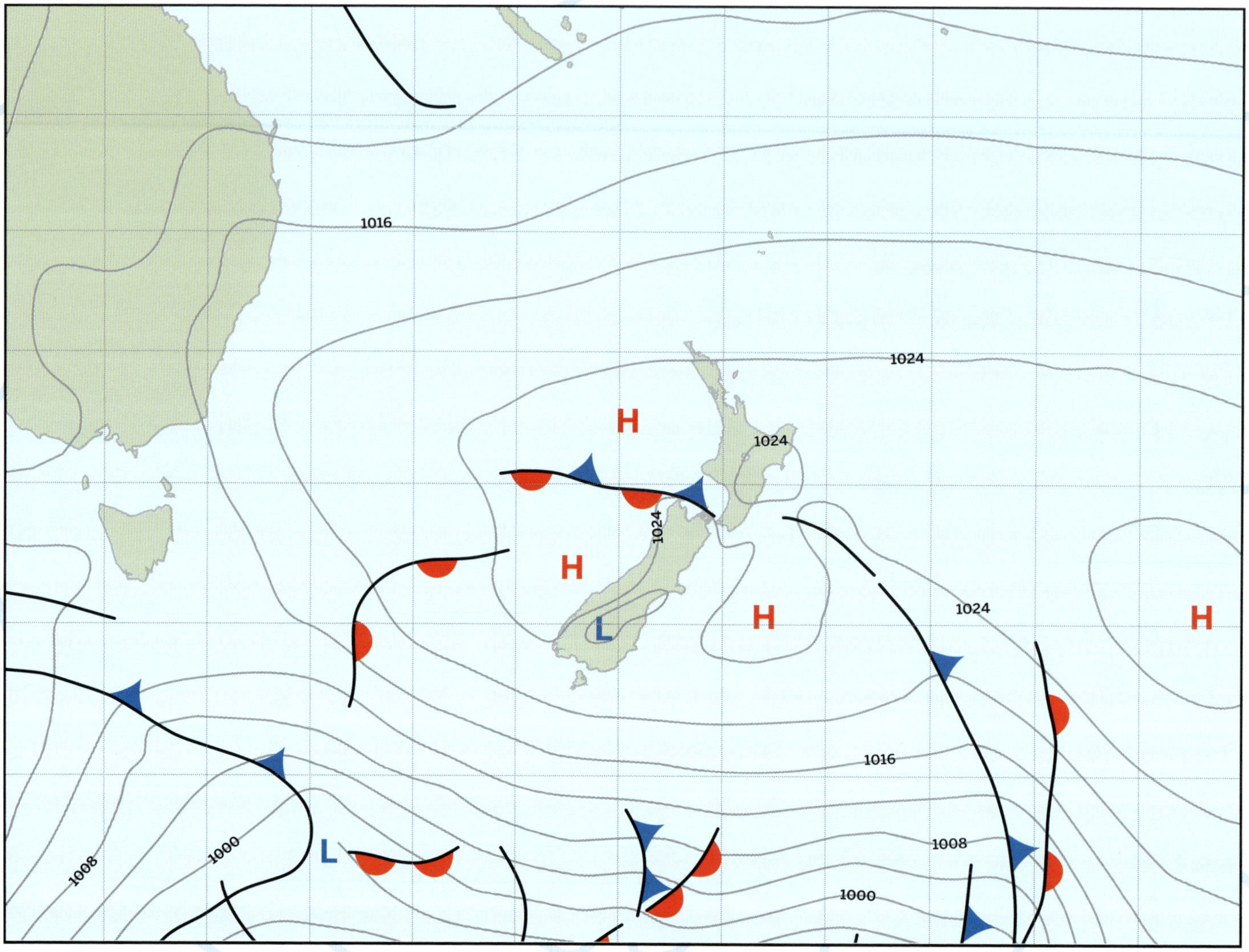
1016
1024
H
1024
1024
H
H
L
1024
H
1016
1008
1000
L
1008
1000

Traditional weather maps show the pattern of air pressure at sea level. Lows (or depressions), are areas where rising air expands and cools, usually bringing rain. Highs (or anticyclones), are associated with sinking air, evaporating cloud and fine weather. Fronts are boundaries between different air masses bringing a change in weather.

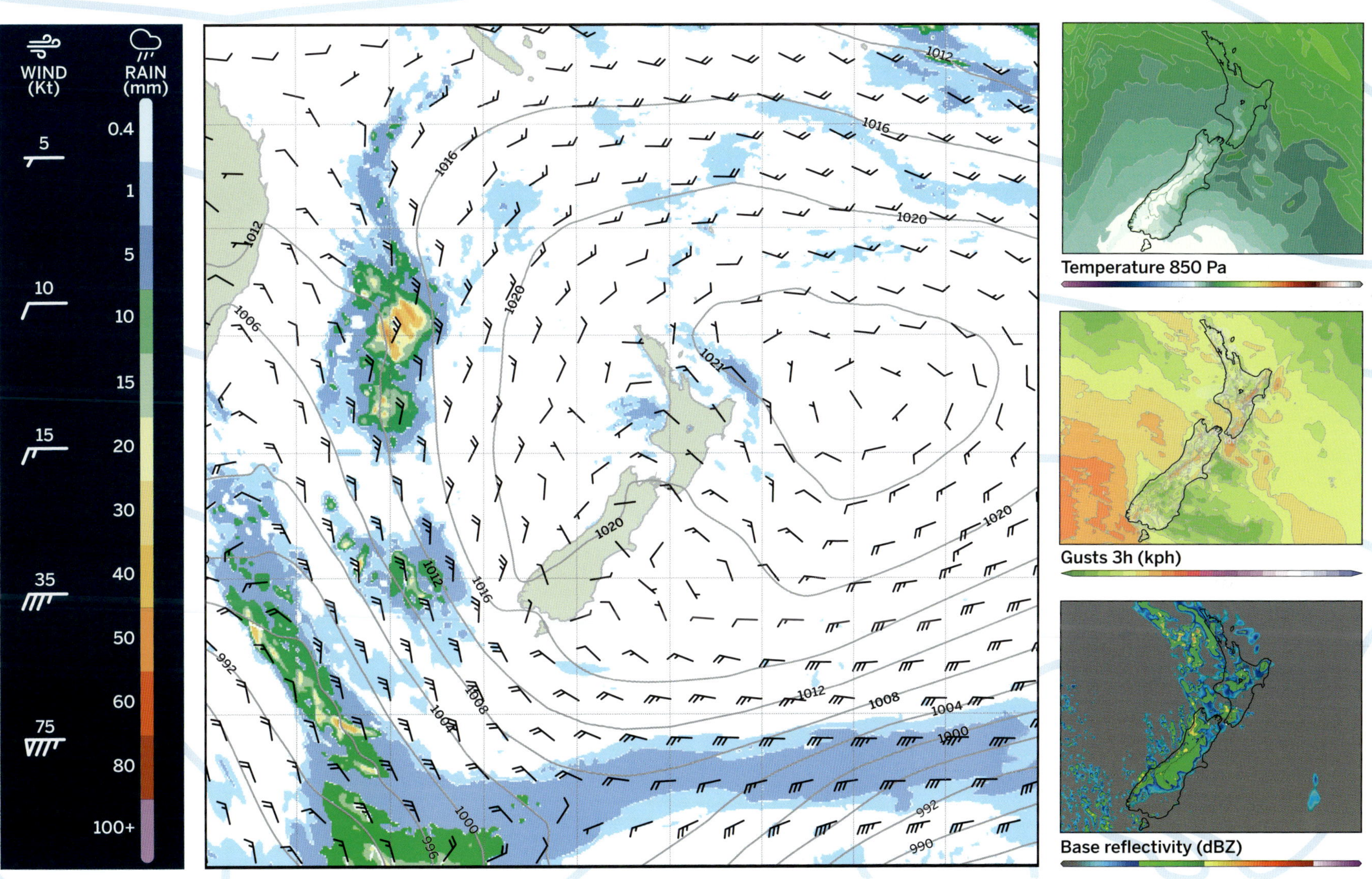

Computer models are now more commonly used as weather predictors. These are created from data which includes satellite imagery and radar. The main map is a rainfall forecast while the smaller images show expected temperature, predicted wind gusts and a radar image of precipitation.

Under correct conditions, air converging towards an area of low pressure will rise. It cools as it does so and the water vapour within it condenses into droplets of water.

These droplets reflect light and we see them as clouds.

If the air is cold enough, clouds may also consist of ice crystals, giving them a different appearance.

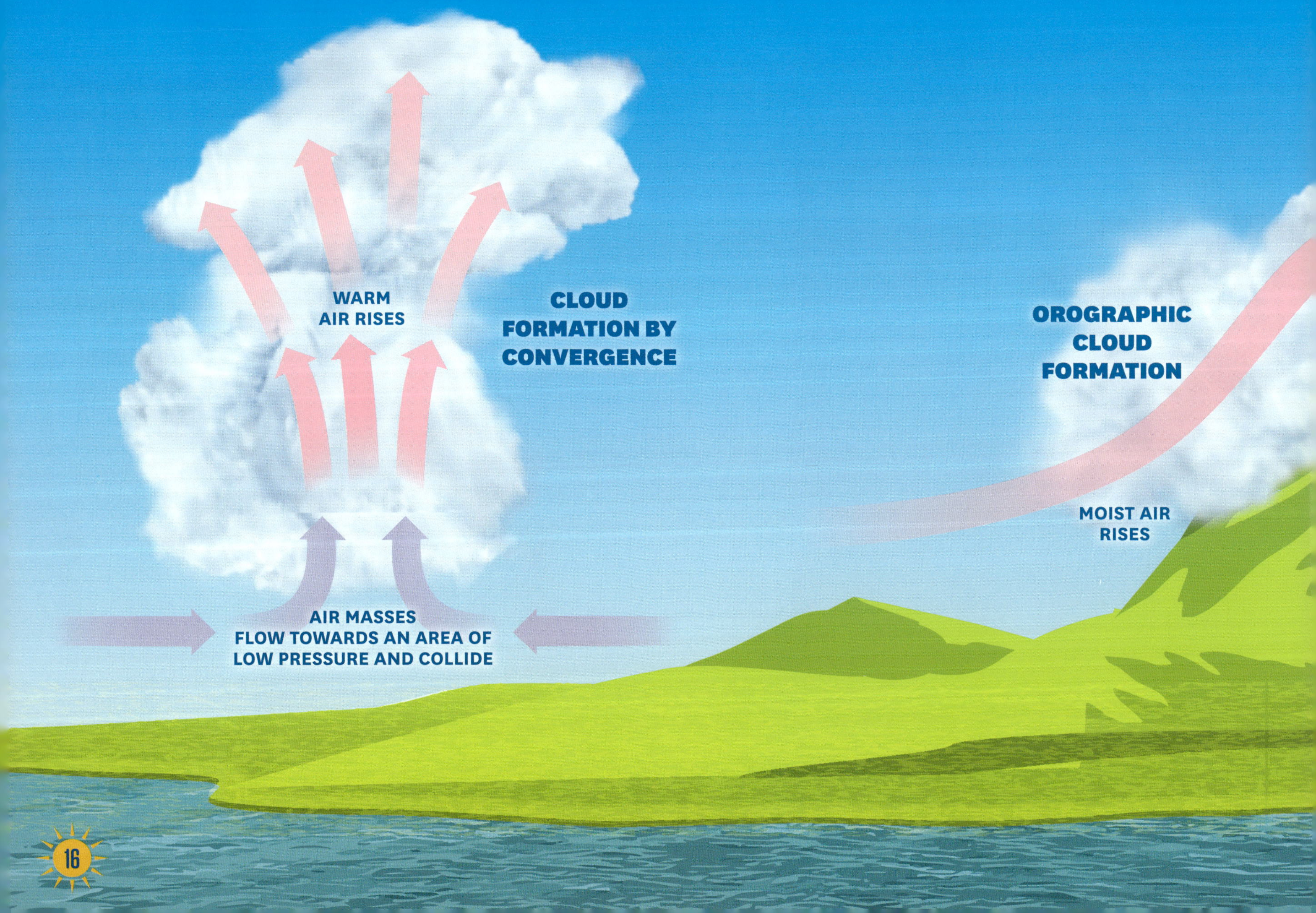

Clouds are categorised into types according to their appearance and position in the lower, middle or upper troposphere.
(See pages 38–39 for a chart of cloud types.)

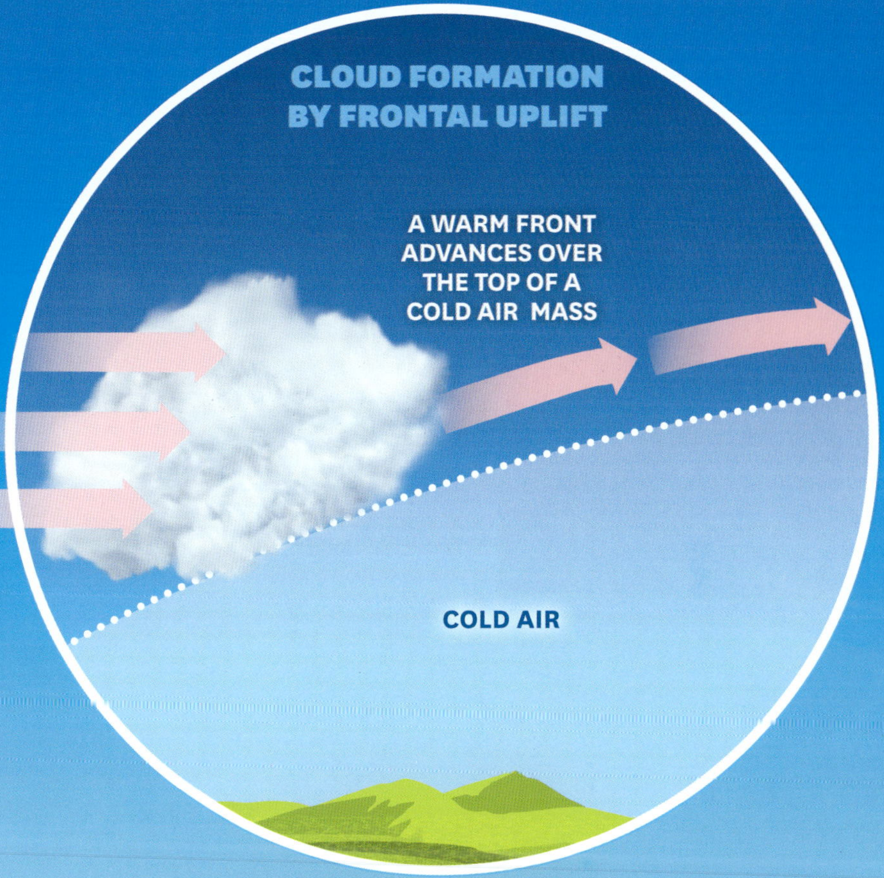

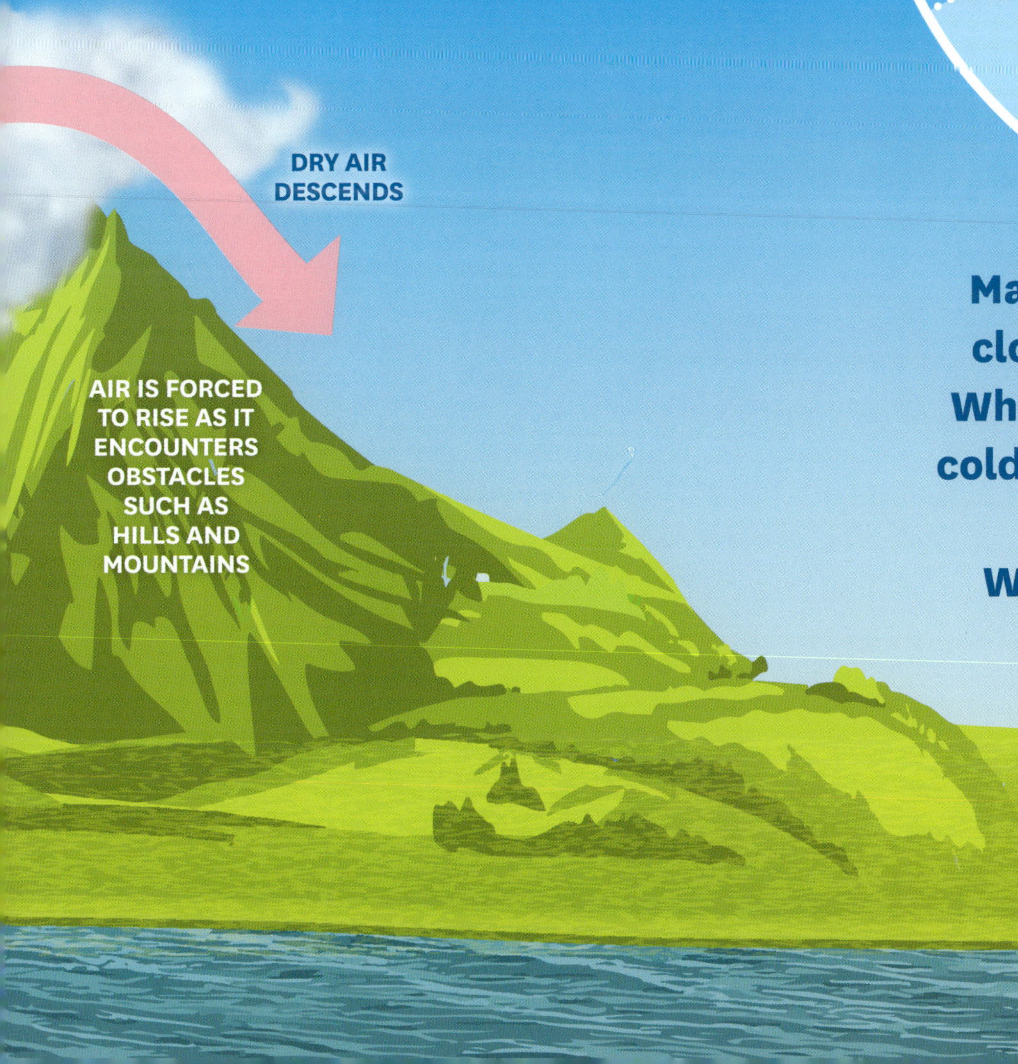

Many of our country's rain-bearing clouds are formed by this process. When a warm air mass approaches a cold one it will ascend over the cooler air, forming a warm front. When a cold air mass approaches a warm one, it wedges under underneath, raising it up.

Inside a cloud, as water droplets collide with others they clump together, gradually increasing in size. Eventually they become too heavy to remain suspended in the cloud and fall towards the ground as precipitation (rain). This is known as the 'warm rain' process.

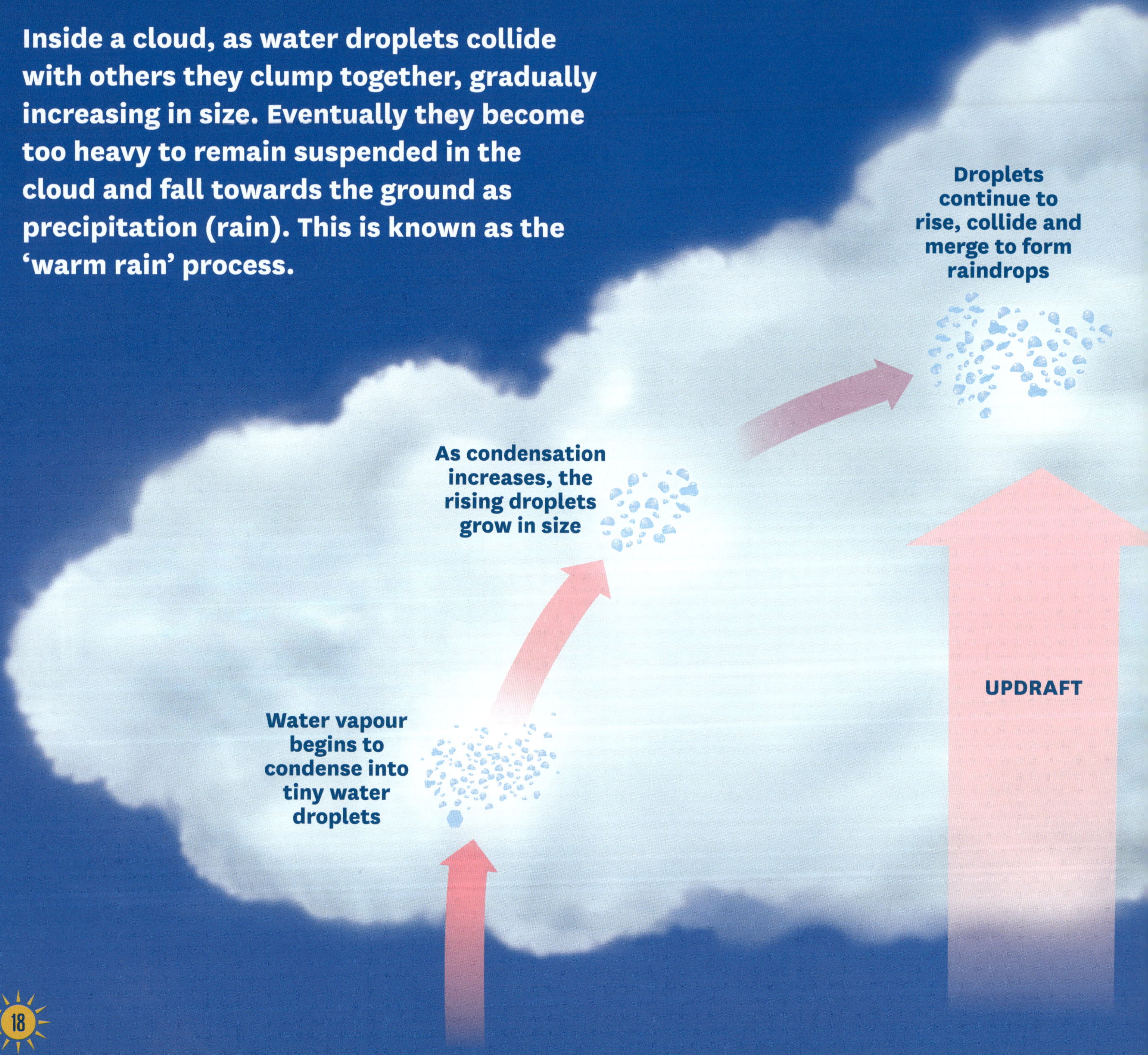

Droplets continue to rise, collide and merge to form raindrops

As condensation increases, the rising droplets grow in size

Water vapour begins to condense into tiny water droplets

UPDRAFT

The appearance of rain is often disappointing because it can sometimes cancel outdoor events and sports, or trips we've been looking forward to. But as well as being necessary for our agricultural and power-generation industries, this process of returning water to the Earth, is crucial for the survival of all life on our planet.

The 'cold rain' process begins at higher, colder altitudes with ice crystals rather than water droplets. These also grow and drop within a cloud, melting into rain while falling through warmer air closer to the ground.

Fog is simply cloud at ground or sea level. It commonly forms overnight, usually in winter, in sheltered valleys or over damp ground, as the Earth cools. It can also occur at any time of the year on hills reaching the cloud layer. Occasionally, fog will drift from the sea onto the land, causing disruption to airports or motorways.

RADIATION FOG

VALLEY FOG

If the temperature of the fog is below zero, the supercooled water droplets within remain liquid but freeze when drifting against a solid object like tree foliage. This deposits a thick layer of 'hoar frost' which can occur in the southernmost parts of the country. Mist is less dense fog which is easier to see through.

Wind pushes warm, moist air across the cool ocean surface, causing the air's water vapour to condense into fog.

ADVECTION FOG

Very warm water causes water vapour in the cooler air above to condense and form a shallow layer above the waves.

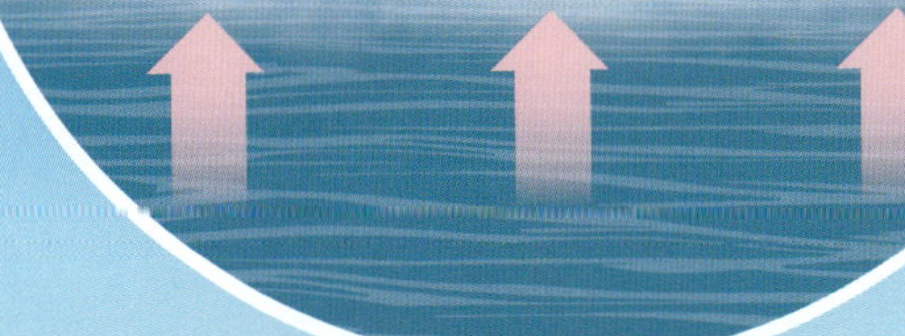

STEAMING FOG

Updraft is the 'engine' of the storm cloud, pulling in moisture and drawing warm, moist air rapidly upward.

Latent heat is produced by the condensation of this air's water vapour, powering the storm.

The 'anvil' shape is formed when the effects of high altitude prevent the cloud growing upward, so it expands outward instead.

Internal currents of air cause water droplets and ice crystals to collide and build up an electrical charge, negative at the base and positive at the top of the cloud. Finally an immense spark is generated within the cloud, or between the cloud and the ground, visible as lightning.

During thunderstorms, the processes which form clouds and produce rain and hail increase in scale and power. Aircraft avoid them because flying near a thunderstorm is a dangerous place to be.
As cold air enters the cloud, it becomes even cooler and more dense.
It then descends back towards the ground, at increased speed.
Thunder is a sonic shockwave generated by a bolt of lightning. A near-instant increase of temperature hotter than the surface of the sun causes the air around it to explosively expand. The resulting detonation is heard as a thunderclap.

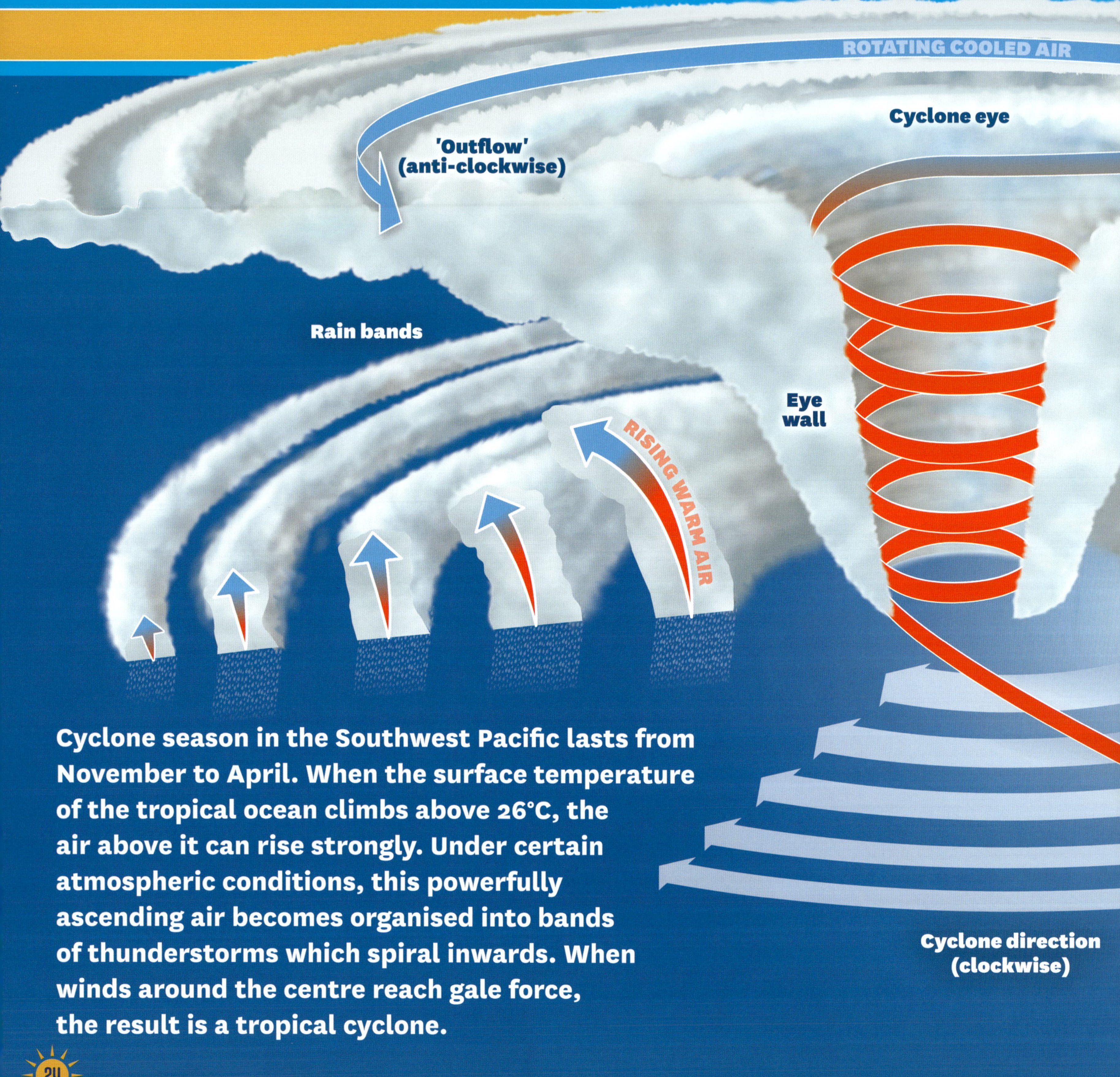

Cyclone season in the Southwest Pacific lasts from November to April. When the surface temperature of the tropical ocean climbs above 26°C, the air above it can rise strongly. Under certain atmospheric conditions, this powerfully ascending air becomes organised into bands of thunderstorms which spiral inwards. When winds around the centre reach gale force, the result is a tropical cyclone.

Cyclone canopy

Rain bands

RISING WARM AIR

Cyclones tend to zig zag across the Pacific like a spinning top on a table, often moving west with the trade winds, and then south-east towards the pole (and sometimes, New Zealand).

Because of their spiralling lines of thunderstorms, and very strong winds near the centre, tropical cyclones pose a threat to anything in their path. Record-breaking rainfall and devastating flooding were recorded over parts of the North Island when Cyclone Gabrielle appeared in 2023.

Southerlies and southwesterlies bring cooler, drier air which has passed across the Southern Ocean to reach New Zealand. If the air has originated over Antarctica we experience a polar outbreak, which usually results in some of our lowest recorded temperatures.

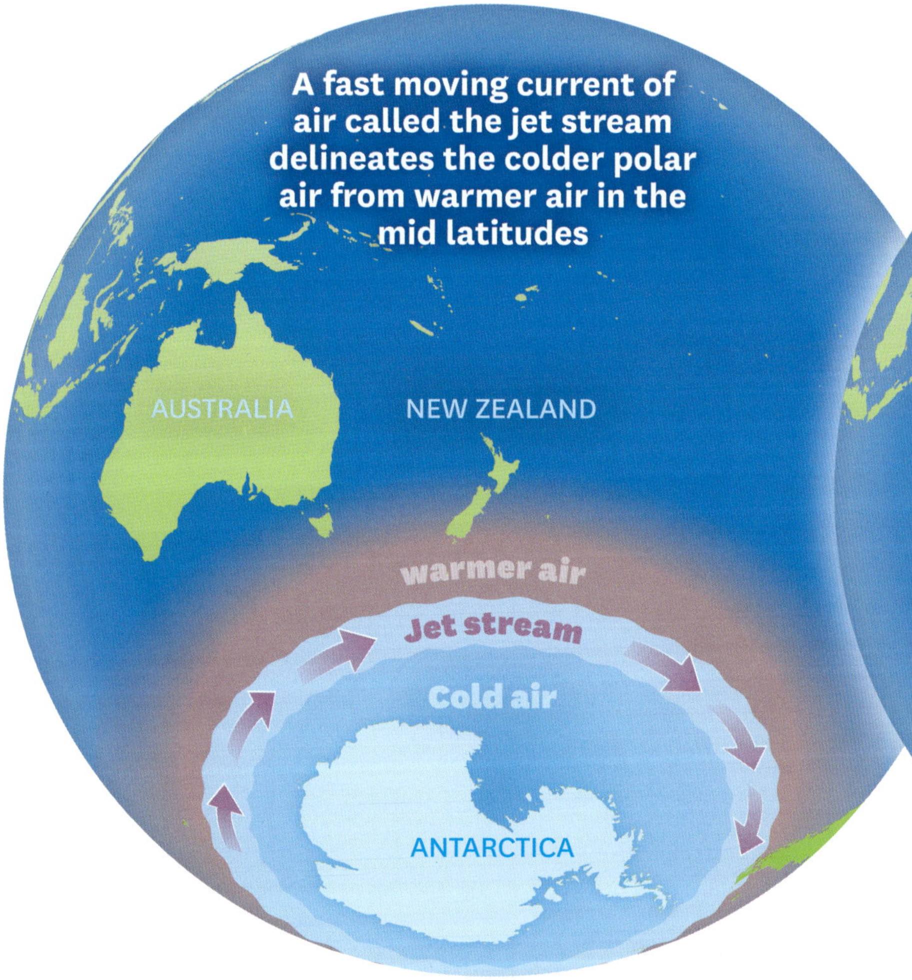

A fast moving current of air called the jet stream delineates the colder polar air from warmer air in the mid latitudes

AUSTRALIA

NEW ZEALAND

warmer air

Jet stream

Cold air

ANTARCTICA

But when it becomes less regular in form, polar air can spread northwards, bringing us colder temperatures

AUSTRALIA

NEW ZEALAND

Jet stream

warmer air

Cold air

ANTARCTICA

Polar outbreaks usually bring snow. In August 2011, a blast of unusually cold air brought snow storms as far as the south and east of the North Island.

SNOW: In the upper, cold parts of a cloud, water vapour freezes into ice crystals (straight to a solid state from gas without becoming liquid first). As they fall they collide and clump together to form snowflakes. (Sleet is rain which contains ice or snow that melts as it falls.)

HAIL: Supercooled water droplets freeze onto condensation nuclei, forming a blob of ice which grows when joined by other freezing droplets. Air trapped between clumped particles give hail stones their white appearance.

SNOW

HAIL

SLEET

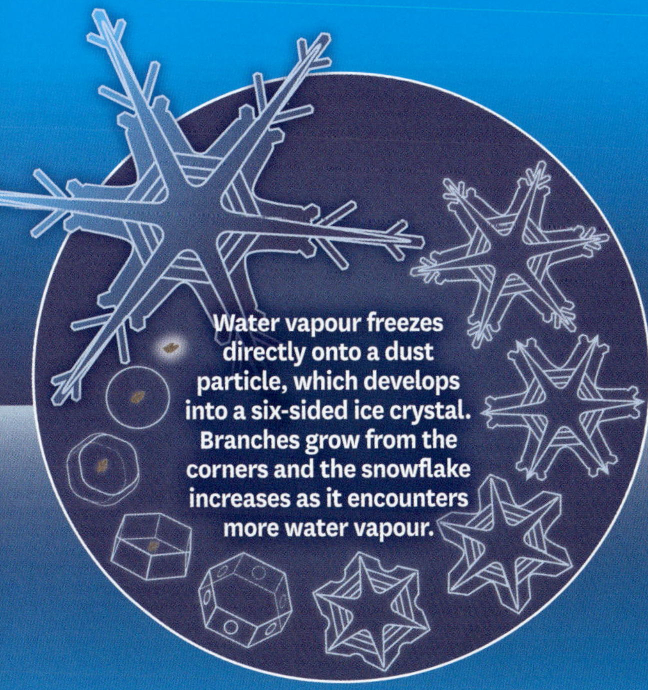

THE FORMATION OF SNOWFLAKES

FROST FORMATION

DEW DROPS CONDENSE

ICE DENDRITES GROW TO FORM FROST LAYER

Having absorbed heat from the sun during the day, the ground releases it again overnight, cooling the air. If conditions are still, water vapour in the air condenses as dew. On a cold, clear night with no cloud to trap heat, ice crystals will form and create frost.

Iwi use a range of natural signs to forecast weather. Te Whānau-ā Apanui Tairāwhiti use the plume of Whakaari/White Island to predict rain or severe conditions.

In the South Island, Kāi Tahu predict rainfall by the appearance of swarms of sandflies, and they mark the early flowering of cabbage trees as an indication of a long hot summer.
Climate change has meant that some traditional signs can no longer be used in the same way. Changes in sea temperature mean that kina are no longer ready for gathering at the traditional time, when pōhutukawa bloom in summer.

Te Reo weather:
paki: ***fine***
wera: ***hot***
makariri: ***cold***
hukapapa: ***snowy***
ua: ***rainy***
marangai: ***stormy***
mākū: wet
tau te kohu: ***foggy***
pupuhi te hau: ***windy***
Kei te mahana: ***warm***

This information is courtesy of the Ministry of Education (Te Tāhuhu o te Mātauranga).

Over billions of years, the Earth's climate has been in constant change. We are currently in the Holocene epoch, which until recently has been a relatively stable period.

However, the rate of change now being measured is more rapid than anything recorded before.
Since the industrial revolution, human consumption of natural resources has steadily produced more greenhouse gases. These include carbon dioxide and methane from the mining and burning of fossil fuels and from waste treatment.

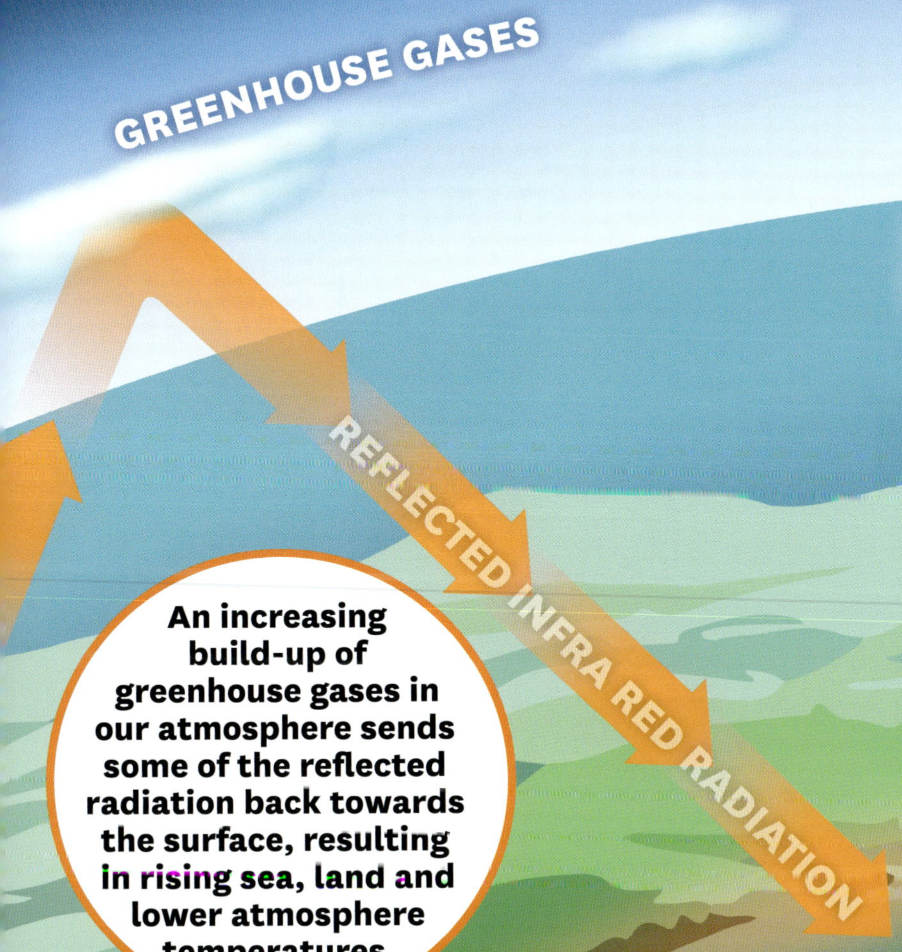

GREENHOUSE GASES

REFLECTED INFRA RED RADIATION

An increasing build-up of greenhouse gases in our atmosphere sends some of the reflected radiation back towards the surface, resulting in rising sea, land and lower atmosphere temperatures.

The global temperature has already risen by 1.2°C, and if we do not change the way we live, further potential increases will bring more extreme weather events, droughts and wildfires, threatening food sources, economies and lives across the world.

It is important not to be discouraged by the consequences of climate change and to remember — thanks to some dedicated individuals and organisations — that humans have joined together to meet challenges to our planet before.

In the 1970s, conservationists protested against the logging of native timber in New Zealand and eventually succeeded in having government policies amended to protect our precious forests.

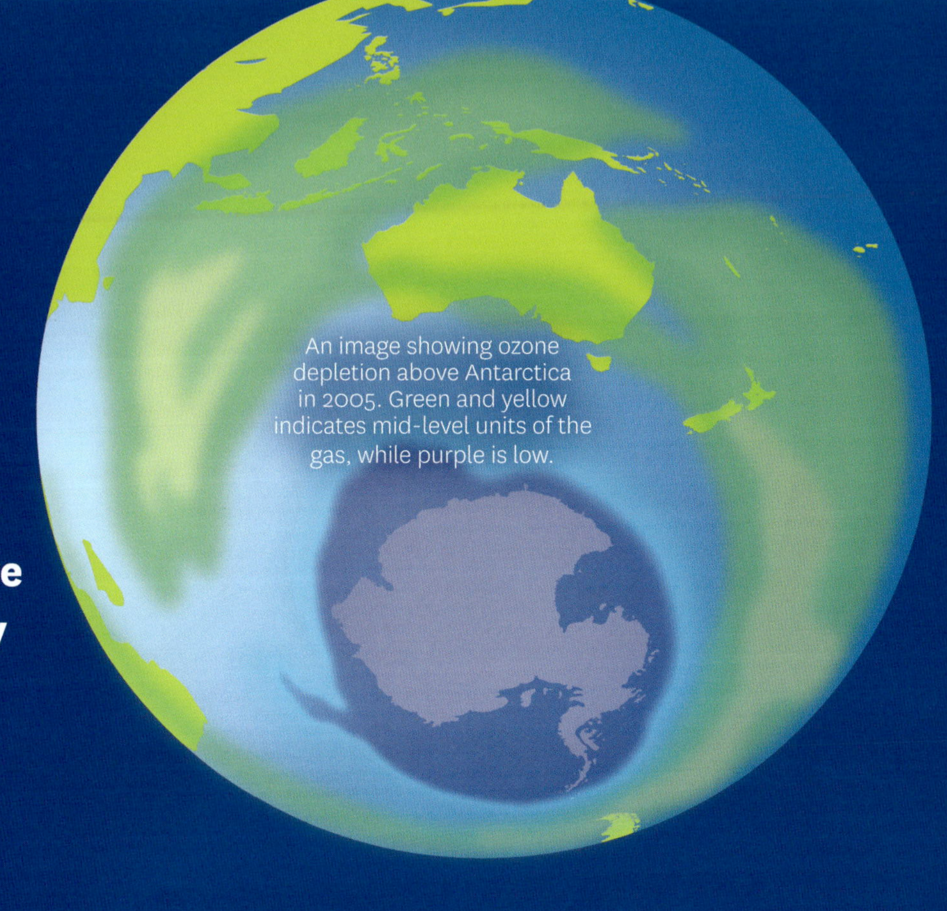

An image showing ozone depletion above Antarctica in 2005. Green and yellow indicates mid-level units of the gas, while purple is low.

In 1987, almost 200 countries signed Montreal protocol, promising to phase out harmful CFC gases which were damaging the ozone layer (a layer high in our atmosphere which shields us from harmful ultraviolet radiation from the sun).

The least damaging ultraviolet rays (UV-A) pass most easily through the ozone layer. UV-B rays can harm the outer-most layers of your skin.

UV-A UV-B UV-C

OZONE LAYER

The World Wildlife Fund (WWF) launched the Climate Heroes project in 2021, in response to climate change. They worked with over 100 young people from Eastern Europe to raise awareness of the climate crisis and launch initiatives to protect our environment. Work continues and many of these young people have become Ambassadors of our Planet and inspire others.

Greta Thunberg

Sir David Attenborough

Other defenders of Earth include young Swedish activist **Greta Thunberg** who challenged world leaders to take immediate action at the UN Climate Conference when she was only 15.

Veteran scientist and broadcaster **Sir David Attenborough** has also campaigned for the protection of our ecosystem for many decades.

Award-winning Kenyan environment activist **Elizabeth Wanjiru Wathuti** founded the Green Generation Initiative which has planted many thousands of tree seedlings in Kenya and encourages young people to discover and care for nature.

Elizabeth Wanjiru Wathuti

Solar energy is the most abundant of all energy resources and can even be harnessed in cloudy weather. 'Going solar' helps the environment — it creates clean, green energy and will assist New Zealand in achieving our target of net zero greenhouse gas emissions by 2050.

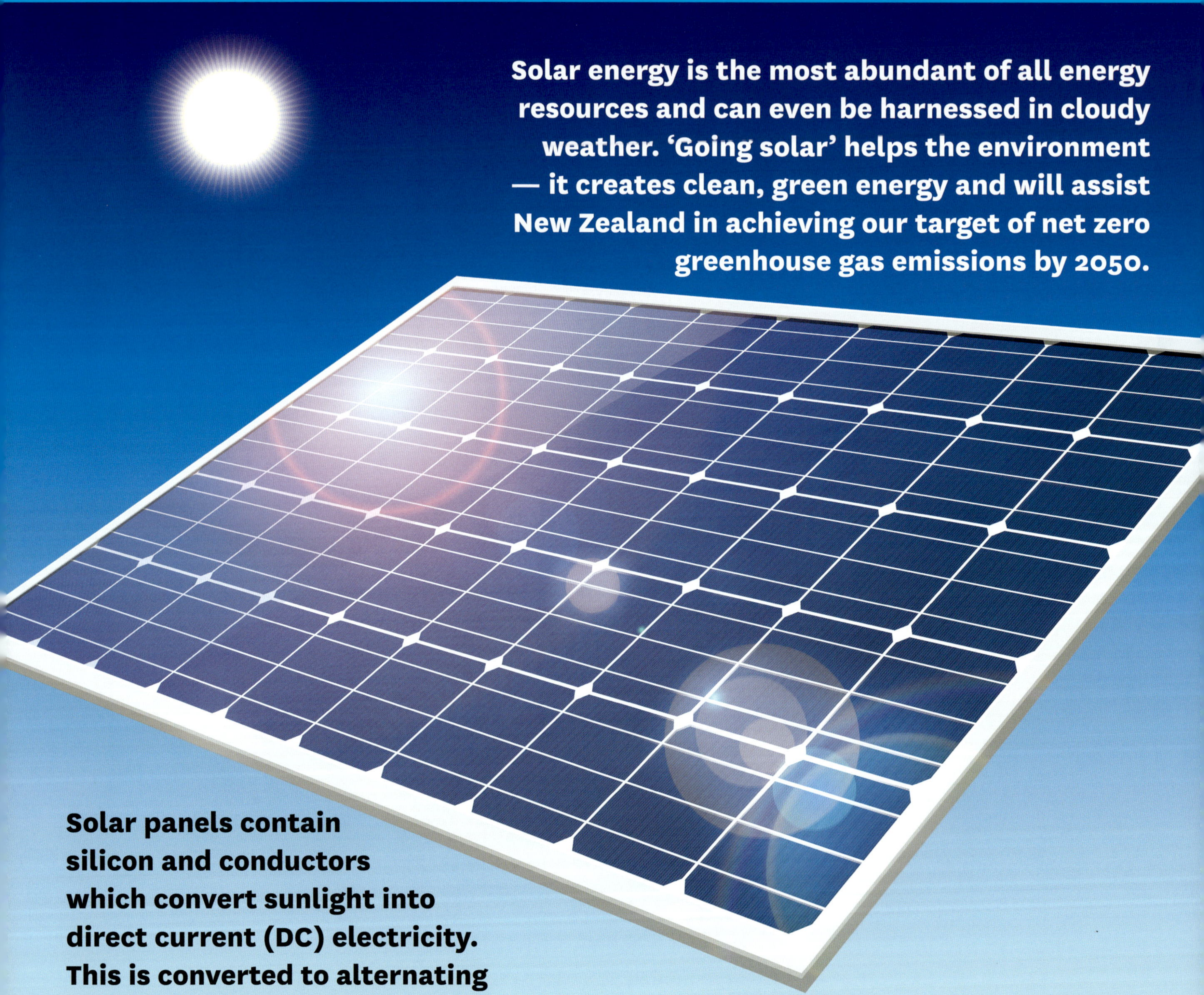

Solar panels contain silicon and conductors which convert sunlight into direct current (DC) electricity. This is converted to alternating current (AC) for household use.

Coal and gas stations emit greenhouse gases as they generate electrical power, losing half the energy used to produce electricity through the production process.

Studies shows that it takes less than six months for a wind farm to produce more energy than it will consume in its entire lifetime.

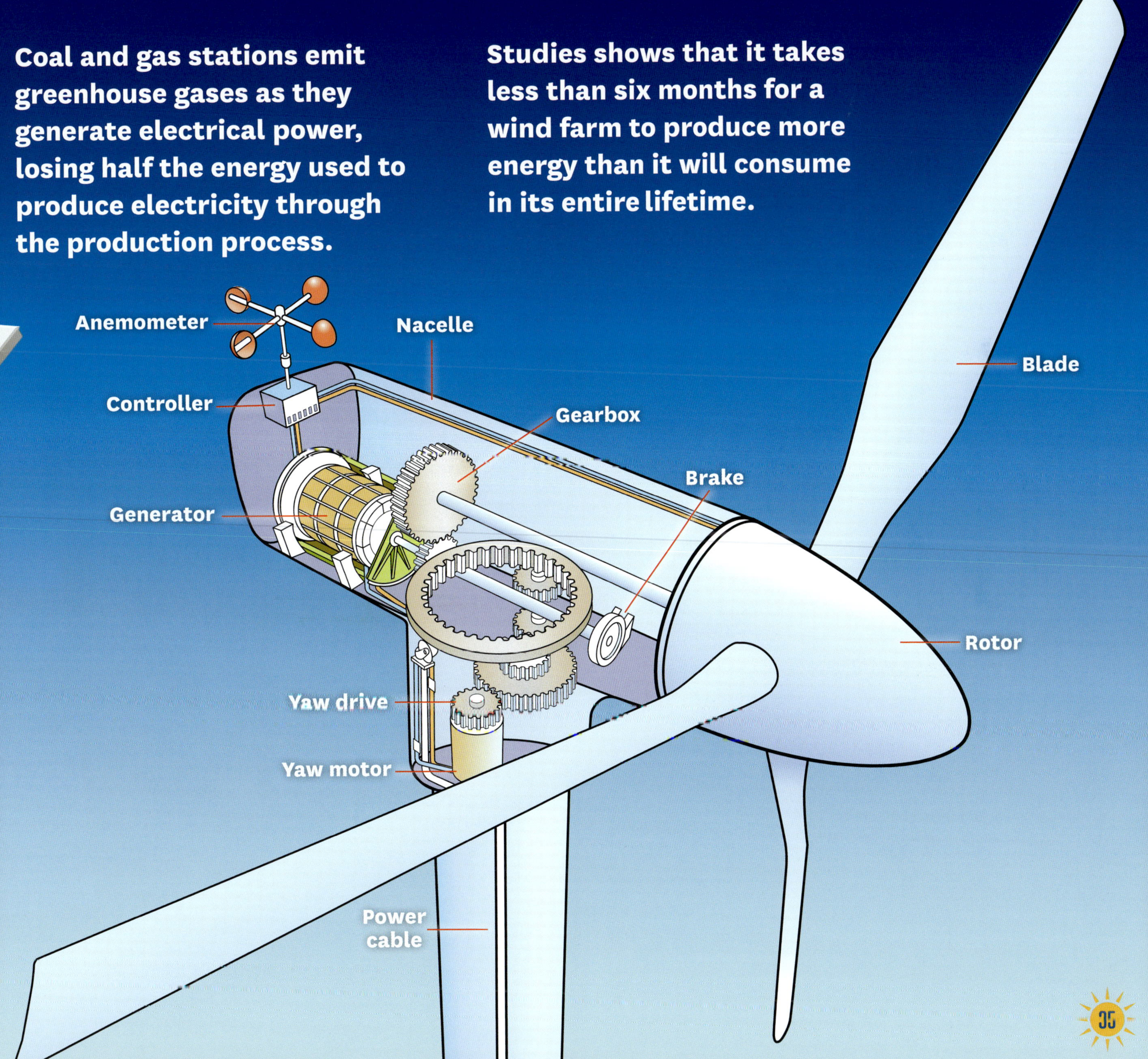

A halo is a ring of light which forms around the sun or moon, as their light is refracted through gently falling ice crystals present in high altitude clouds.

The crystals behave like mirrors and prisms, splitting and scattering light outwards in a ring, if distributed randomly.

A sun pillar is a vertical column of light extending from the setting or rising sun. If conditions are very calm and high-altitude ice crystals have settled in formation, they reflect a shaft of sunlight upwards into the sky.

SUNLIGHT

RAINDROP

Sunlight entering a raindrop is refracted (split into rainbow colours), and reflected off the back of the droplet, refracted again as it travels to your eye.

SUN PILLAR

SUN DOG (Parhelia)

Ice crystals can also produce 'sun dogs' (also called parhelia). These appear as a bright spot on either, or both sides of the sun.

A corona is formed by another process acting upon light, called diffraction. Unlike the hollow ring of a halo it appears as a 'filled' circle about the sun or moon.

This is a magnified image of the sun or moon caused by light being 'bent' through tiny ice crystals and water droplets, then cast onto a thin cloud layer.

THE GREEN FLASH

Green flashes only occur under the perfect atmospheric conditions, making them very rare. As the sun sets, the atmosphere refracts sunlight into its various colours. We see the reddish colours most because they have a longer wavelength, and the bluish colours are scattered. A mirage at the horizon (caused by a layer of lower density warm air) can intensify the last colour visible: green, making it visible as a flash in the last moment of the sunset.

Cirrostratus
Cirrocumulus
Cirrus
Altostratus
Altocumulus
Altocumulus
Lenticularis
nimbostratus
Stratus
Cumulus
Stratocumulus

Clouds are classified according to their altitude and appearance.

High-level clouds occur around 7,000 metres in the sky and have the prefix 'cirro' (which means 'curl of hair').

Due to the cold upper atmosphere, they are mainly composed of ice crystals.

The three main types of high clouds are cirrus, cirrostratus, and cirrocumulus.

Mid-level clouds are given the prefix 'alto' (meaning 'mid'), and form between 2,000 and 7,000 m up.

They consist of liquid water droplets and ice crystals, and the two main types are altostratus and altocumulus.

Lenticular altocumulus can not only form distinctive 'saucer-shaped' clouds, but also the familiar northwest arch.

Low-level clouds are not given a prefix, instead their names are derived from 'strato' (layer), 'cumulo' (heap), or 'nimbo' (rain), depending on their appearance. They form below 2,000 m, and are usually made up of liquid water droplets, turning to ice crystals and snow during winter storms.

Cumulonimbus storm clouds extend through all levels.

Cumulonimbus

A catalogue record for this book is available from the National Library of New Zealand

ISBN 978-1-77694-081-3
A White Cloud Book
Published in 2025 by Upstart Press Ltd
26 Greenpark Road, Penrose, Auckland 1061
New Zealand

Design and Illustration by Alistair Hughes

Printed by Everbest

Acknowledgements

Thanks to Rose, my only sunshine

and my parents, Bernard and Jean, for bringing me to this beautiful country.